# 7- Stage Parenting

## Jon Freeman

## How to meet your child's changing needs

*Published by Spiralworld, Salisbury*

© Jon Freeman, Salisbury UK, 2019

All rights reserved. No part of this work may be reproduced without written permission from Jon Freeman, except for brief quotations.

www.spiralworld.net

Other information available on www.accesstopossibility.net

Available in print, audio and Kindle formats

ISBN: 978-0993-3192-3-5  Paperback

ISBN: 978-0993-3192-4-2  Kindle / E-book

An earlier draft of this material was published in 2012 under the title "7-step parenting".

## Contents

Learning to Parent ............................................................................... 1

There's no such thing as..... ............................................................... 3

Nature or Nurture: What makes us who we are? ......................... 5

Why Seven stages?  The Human Development Spiral ................... 8

    Beige: Parent as incubator ........................................................ 11

    Purple: Parent as Tribal Chief .................................................. 14

    Red: Parent as Border Patrol ................................................... 22

    Blue: Parent as Rule-maker ...................................................... 29

    Orange: Parent as Manager ..................................................... 39

    Green: Parent as Guide and Mentor ....................................... 47

    The Yellow Stage: Entry into Second Tier: Parents as friends ........... 52

Postscript 1: A note about time ........................................................ 56

Postscript 2: Teaching children about choices ............................... 57

Biography.  A bit about Jon Freeman ............................................. 60

Acknowledgements etc. ..................................................................... 61

# Learning to Parent

Few of us are taught how to be parents. It may be the most important thing that we ever do, the one with greatest long-lasting impact on another individual and the one with most potential to build a vibrant human future, but I wasn't taught it in school. It would be unusual if you were different.

I have a picture in my mind – a cartoon with four frames. In each frame you see three women, sitting together in a family room. They are visibly grandma, mother and an adult daughter with an infant girl on her lap.

In frame one, grandma is speaking. She says "My mother was very loving and very close. I felt suffocated and determined that I would not do that to any daughter of mine".

In frame two, mother is saying to grandma "I felt you were distant, and that you didn't give me enough warmth and affection. I was determined to make my daughter feel loved and cherished."

In frame three, the adult daughter is turned to her mother, saying "Gee mom, I know you love me, but can't you give me a little space! I can't breathe here." Frame 4 shows the infant screaming.

* * *

This little book is about some simple pointers to what children need, how that changes as they develop, and about the learning journey we take together with our children.

What it won't cover:

- When to potty train

- When to allow your child a smartphone
- How to decide what screen time your child should have
- How to discuss online pornography with your 10-year old

The above list contains a few examples among hundreds of difficult choices and challenging issues.  I don't have answers for these, or many, many others.  Often there are no "right" answers, whatever your grandmothers or mothers-in-law may believe.  They are your personal and shared choices, dependent on who you are, who your child is and what you know and sense about the relationship.

With all of these choices, I wish you patience, kindness and listening; the courage to follow your heart; the confidence to trust in your instincts; understanding, wisdom and love.   And all the good fortune the universe can offer.

# There's no such thing as…..

Here's some bad news. It is impossible to be a perfect parent.

> **There's no such thing as a perfect parent**

Actually, I look on that as good news. The moment that you get the truth of that statement, you are relieved of the obligation to try for perfection. Hopefully you can relax a little. More good news is that you don't need to be perfect, and neither does your child.

I am not a doctor. I cannot tell you about the best way to treat measles. Even the paper qualifications that I do have are not related to parenting. My qualifications, such as they are, consist of having two biological children and a stepchild, plus 40 adult years of being a parent and observing others. I have spent a couple of years organising a co-operative home-school for 14-16 year olds. I am a Trustee of a Charity which provides care and education to learning disabled children. By profession I am a consultant in organisational change, a leadership development coach and a trainer in Spiral Dynamics. It's a rag-bag background from which to talk about parenting.

On the other hand, doctors may not be experts in education, teachers are not developmental psychologists and there is no certainty that any of them were fully engaged in raising children. So I may have a wider viewpoint than all of them.

Here is another piece of good news. There is no-one who can tell you how to raise your child. No such expert exists. Even if I had degrees in medicine, paediatrics, psychology, psychiatry and the Wisdom of Solomon too, I couldn't tell you what to do when your baby wakes up at 3am, your 6-year-old refuses to go to bed or your teen is dumped by their first girlfriend.

The reason why that is good news is that it sets you free. You are an individual and so is your child. What happens between you is unique. It grows from who the two of you are. That principle expands to embrace co-parents, siblings and wider families. The whole thing is unrepeatable.

Since you can't be a perfect parent, and there is no greater expert on your child, I hope you can see the sense in the following conclusion. **You will have to trust yourself**. Learn to trust your instincts and your connection.

Trust that it is much harder to cause lasting damage than you may well fear.

Trust that even with the "cartoon" four generations, all are still in the room with one another, and all are talking about it. Within the quality of relational trust and trustworthiness resides the potential for learning from and with each other -- no matter what happens along the way. Here, we are exploring what contributes to the increased likelihood for such an outcome.

# Nature or Nurture: What makes us who we are?

There has been a debate for two thousand years or more on a very big question. Are we born as a kind of blank slate, on which life writes everything that we become? Or do we come into the world with something predetermined, and if so, what? Where is the balance?

I don't propose to debate that scientifically but I want you to know where I stand, because it frames everything in this book. Everything that I have seen convinces me that children arrive with some kind of personality or character. You can ascribe this to their horoscope, their past lives and karma, their family genetics, to ancestral memories. You can believe in pre-birth soul choices and destiny, or you can see all of these possibilities as nonsense because it's just random chance. But whatever the cause, I encourage you to accept my view that your child has come in with something of its own. You may have already noticed that anyway.

> There is a story about two businessmen talking about their upcoming weekend, and one is saying to the other "I am taking my son to the baseball game". "But you hate baseball", says the other. "Yes", comes the reply. "But I love him, and he's into baseball right now."

It is entirely possible for a child to be born with a huge talent for something that you know nothing about – like the great jazz pianist Errol Garner. He never learned to read music because there was no-one to teach him.

This works both ways. Half of my family were professional musicians and so, for a short while, was I. None of my children are. If you have ambitions for your child, hold them lightly. Very lightly. They probably have ambitions of their own. Share your passions with them, whether it's basketball or crochet – let them hear and feel the joy of having something they love to do. Richard Feynman, a Nobel-winning physicist on a level with Einstein – was filled by his father with enthusiasm and curiosity that never left him. But he was never pushed to be anything. Let them find their own passion.

Inside this story is the general principle that being a parent is about both teaching and learning. You will learn who your child is, whether you like it or not. From Day One, she will impose herself on your life. She will shape you. It is a two-way street. It's easier if you accept that from the start.

That does not mean that you abandon all thoughts of influence. Even if you believe that this new relationship is random, I encourage you to behave **as if** this child has chosen you to be its parent – that they have come to have the experiences that **only you** can give them, and to learn from who you are. See it as a mutual process. And if you can behave as if you have drawn this individual into your life because of what he has to teach you, it will help too. But we will come to that.

Ultimately, like much of life, being a parent will be about balance. It is nature <u>and</u> nurture. It is teaching <u>and</u> learning. It is doing our best <u>and</u> learning how to treat everything as perfect. In that sense, you **are** the perfect parent, even when you can just see that you made a mistake. Your child **is** a perfect child, even when you have just grounded them for something unacceptable. The world is full of people who have done magnificent things because of what they learned from their misspent youth.

The poet Philip Larkin wrote "They mess you up, your mum and dad. They may not mean to, but they do." Actually, his language was more robust but that's the sense of it. We have to learn to live with the paradox that everything is perfect and nothing is perfect. So the rest of this book is not about perfect parenting, but it is about some fundamentals of human development that should help you to understand and enjoy the journey that you and your child are taking. It might even help you view your own journey and your own parents in a fresh light.

# Why Seven stages? The Human Development Spiral

Most of what follows is based on a theory which has come to be known as "Spiral Dynamics". Originally formulated by Dr Clare W. Graves, this is a very deep and powerful view of human development through the ages. It encompasses biology, psychology and social behaviour and maps the changing relationship that we humans have with the conditions that we live in. In my view it is as powerful in that sphere as Darwin's theory of evolution is in relation to the emergence of species. But the parenting part is simpler than that and works by itself.

CLARE W. GRAVES:

Technically, Graves' theory is about adult development over historical time. In presenting a spiral-related view of children, I am extending the theory into places which are not justified by his original research. I do so with a clear conscience, because what I am about to say corresponds closely with my experience and connects well with other views of children such as those from Piaget or Rudolf Steiner. It is also connected with an academic paper that I have published.[1] I hope that he would have approved.

---

[1] Freeman, J. (2018). A Developmental View of the Personal Psychological Journey. *Journal of Experiential Psychotherapy*, 21 (3), 3-21.

https://jep.ro/images/pdf/cuprins_reviste/83_art_1.pdf

Above all, it works. The stages which Graves recognised in adults don't arrive in humans from outside. They exist as potentials, as capacities we are born with and which our life experiences call upon and draw out from us. Our job as parents is to help these capacities to be present in our children so that they can meet life's varied challenges. The acorn contains the oak it is to be. It is shaped by wind and sunlight. Your job is to provide food and water, and to expose your sapling to the light.

By nature, a Spiral is a continuous thread, as it is in the diagram below. The stages which we will work with are useful landmarks in the journey. However, they do not pop up suddenly; rather they are a continuum of transition. Our children will not suddenly leap into a stage and they will not lose what went before. Each one emerges and may also at times recede, for reasons which I will explain. This flexibility and the gradual nature of the change makes it easier to work with.

At the same time, for convenience we describe the stages as if they are distinct and you will find them recognisable, in your own children and others. If you take the time to do so, you may also be able to look back at your own life and see them reflected in your journey and you may also get some insight into how these different ways of being show up in you now, as an adult. Part of the convenience in how we describe the stages is that each has a designated colour. You don't need to know why they were chosen and it is worth saying that they don't correspond with any other system. The choice is of low significance and doesn't affect how you apply these methods.

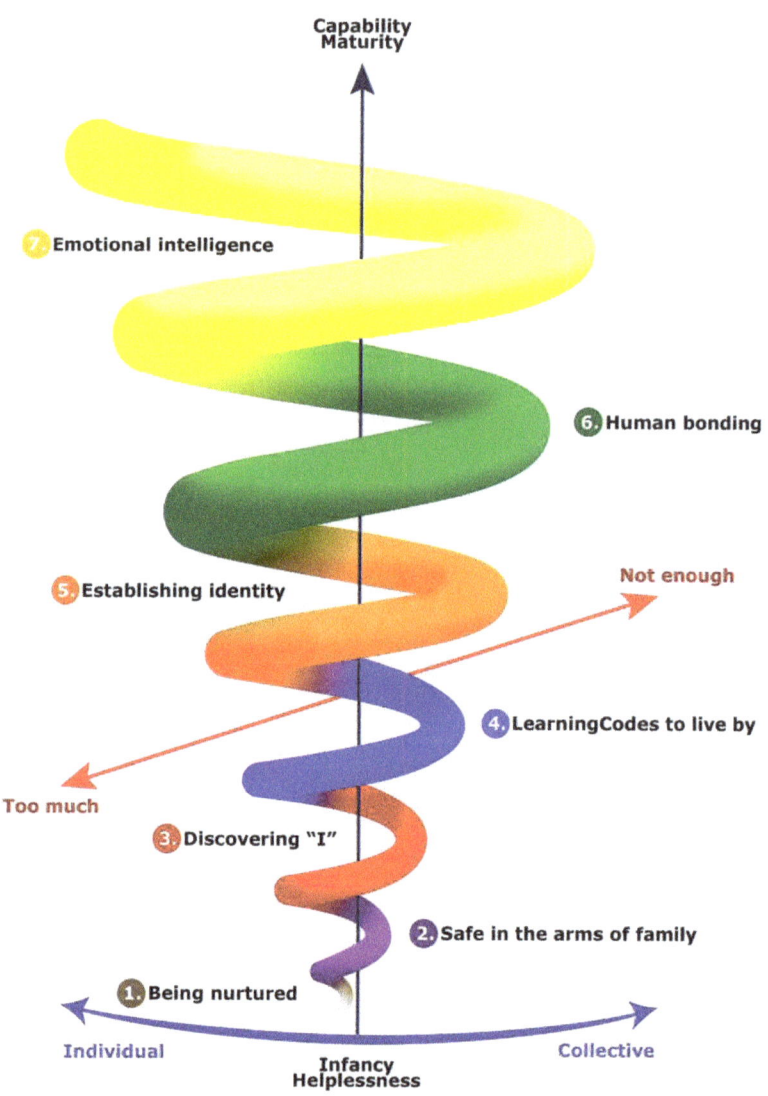

We are called upon to be seven different kinds of parent.

## Beige: Parent as incubator

The first humans to evolve existed in small bands, as hunter-gatherers, without technology or settled agriculture. They were just one step up from chimpanzees. Their life conditions were very challenging. On a daily basis their needs were for food, water, shelter and safety from predators. So the primary Values and priorities for humans in those conditions are related to **survival** needs.

It does not take much imagination for us to see the new-born infant in this light. We are just about the most helpless new-born of any species. Kittens may be born blind but they do not stay that way for long; we remain in a helpless state for months. Your baby depends on you for everything and there is nothing else to be done but to take care of those needs. Keep them moderately warm and free from harm, feed when hungry, clean when soiled and comfort when distressed. It's as simple as that.

And of course it isn't quite that simple in practice. We face a number of challenges. To start with we don't always know what the baby needs. She's fed, cleaned, warmly clothed and still she's crying. We have a biological response to infant crying – a powerful inbuilt program that wants it to stop.

There are many theories about why babies cry – that they are exercising their lungs, releasing hurts from their birth experience, missing the familiarity of the womb or even wishing that they were back in the bliss of pre-incarnation spiritual oneness. Whatever you believe, you will not always know why. But from day one, it helps to establish an empathic connection with the baby. You might think of this as intuitive, as spiritual, as in the realm of unconscious emotions. If you are a mother, the baby is used to being close, living within the rhythmic and electromagnetic field of your heart. But that field is detectable several metres from the body, so even if you are a father, the baby will normally have felt your field too. He knows when you are agitated and when you are calm. Beige uses **instinct** as part of its survival kit.

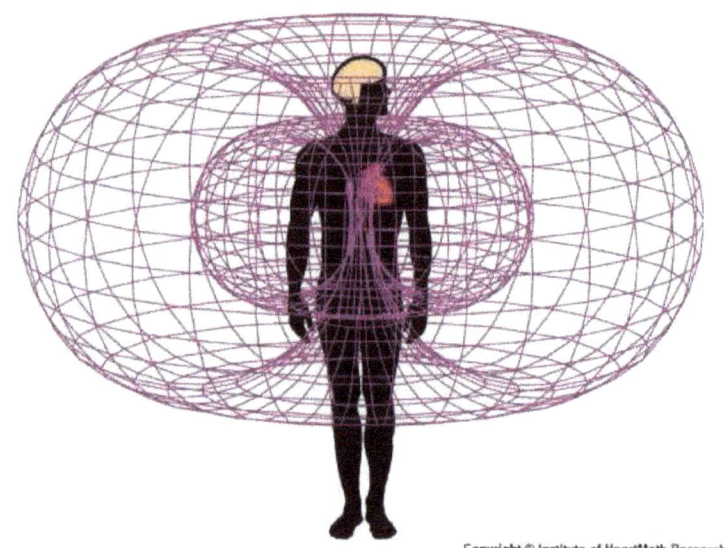
Copyright © Institute of HeartMath Research Center

Many people will offer you advice, often based on personal experience, sometimes even wise, but none of them will know. I encourage you to listen to your baby – the deep listening that you would use for prayer or meditation. Often that connection, that holding will bring stillness. Some babies are naturally secure enough to be put down. Others are not. You will need to find your own balance. Babies love contact, and many traditional societies would see the baby carried in a shawl or sling next to mother's body for months, extending a womblike experience, rocked by the motion of activity, hearing her voice, feeling her presence. Modern society and lifestyles do not make that easy to do, but most infants will love it if you can.

If I have learned one thing above all about infants, it is that they are not as fragile as they look. In fact they are really pretty tough, both physically and psychologically. Look around the world and see what conditions they adapt to. They get used to things. Do what you can. Notice what works for your baby and what doesn't. Learn with him. But above all don't worry. He can feel your anxiety. So when you have done everything that you can think of and it hasn't stopped the crying, just connect and be with him. He's

OK. Breathe deeply, and trust. The Beige survival stage doesn't stay dominant forever. The sleepless nights will pass. Enjoy the connection.

## Purple: Parent as Tribal Chief

*I don't need a big vacation*

*I would just like the bathroom to myself once in a while*

Mere Beige survival was a raw existence. As humans became better at it and numbers grew, the conditions were created where it became possible to band together in larger numbers for **safety and stability**. The possibility developed for a tribal existence, with wider relationships, greater security against the competition with other humans and with the possibility to build knowledge through **tradition and elder wisdom**, so that Beige survival needs were underpinned by group efforts.

For the infant there is a gradual widening of their sphere of perception. At birth, her needs are immediate, all-consuming, and biological. As parent, you are an extension of herself; you are the part of her that meets those needs.

Some of this continues, even as she begins to crawl and to explore the world. The process of mastering the physical world is a long one for humans. A calf is walking within hours. We take a couple of years to develop the body size, the physical strength and the co-ordination that enables such a big brain to be transported upright on two legs.

Mastery of the environment is also about knowledge, but this is not intellectual understanding. Children are learning how life works, but this is a magical, mysterious experience. They spend a great deal of time watching and listening. Don't be misled into thinking that nothing is happening. They observe; they copy. They learn language. They will take on your habits and will love familiarity and routine – the song that is sung over and again, the story that never loses its appeal. Dad, your son will speak to his mother the same way that you do. You are still an extension of who he is, because in the Tribe, the individual is subsumed in the group. For a child at this stage, the family and its environment is the entire world, and that world is surrounded by mystical and magical beings – including Father Christmas and the tooth fairy. The sun has a big smiley face; Mickey Mouse and teddy-bear are as real as each other. Psychological safety depends on all of them and you threaten this reality at your peril. Many parents have two of the child's favourite soft toy so that it isn't a trauma when one is in the laundry. To throw it away will be seen forever as unforgivable (I know a woman in her fifties who never lost her upset at her mother for doing so) and you may know other adults who still have theirs.

In this stage, Mom and Dad are the tribal chief and shaman. They carry the wisdom of the tribe. This magical safety in a big and threatening world is a foundational element for healthy development. It is very easy in our complex and technical world to think that children need to learn early about what is, or is not real. We may also think, because of the pressure around educational achievement, that children should already be "learning".

This attitude will not support your child, and will actually be counter-productive. In the Purple phase you are building the linings for what is to come. If you try to push ahead on this learning curve, the gaps will show up later. Einstein was a genius first and foremost because he could imagine something that no-one else could and is well-known for speaking very little at this age. Purple is where creative imagination is fostered or suppressed.

Asking your child to learn is going too far in one direction. Benign neglect is the opposite. I don't mean to be preachy, but since the central theme of this stage is bonding, I encourage you to be aware of how easy it is to become disconnected. Strollers and pushchairs where your child faces away from you can be isolating. You might at least need to make sure you are talking to them so that they can feel you there.

## Brainwaves

There is science behind what I am saying here, and it is about brain wave frequency.

Up to two years old, the human brain functions primarily in the range of 0.5 to 4 cycles per second. This band is known as **Delta waves**. It is the level that you go to in deep sleep. For the infant, it relates initially to how much they actually do sleep. But even when a 1-year-old is awake, they are functioning primarily from their subconscious.

Information from the outside world receives little in the way of critical thinking or editing. The thinking, conscious mind is operating at a very low level at this age.

Don't let this fool you into thinking that no intelligence is in operation. What takes place is pattern-sensing, a more instinctive accumulation of information. A 1-year-old draws conclusions about what they are seeing that they could not yet verbalise, but which are clear in experimental observations.

Delta also underlies the early development of imagination and creativity. Since language and conceptual thinking is not yet available, the word "image" which sits inside "imagination", is central to the way the brain is operating. This is equally relevant to what adults describe as "magical thinking". Real images and those contained in myths and stories have equal weight.

> Lastly, please be aware that there is strong evidence that the Beige and Purple systems support human access to the realm of intuition and sensitivity to aspects of non-material reality. For example, your child may know your thoughts before you have said them; this can be particularly strong in children on the autistic spectrum (see *resources). Conventional science does not recognise these assertions, but they have their own evidence base and scientific rationale. I have written of this in depth in my book "The Science of Possibility". I understand if these statements are challenging to your way of thinking because we are nearly all trained to something else. I can only encourage you to keep an open, curious and observing mind to your child's experience.

The next thing to be aware of is how you use your mobile phone / mp3 device. It is all too easy for it to become a habit that when you are out walking, a conversation with someone else seems more interesting, or you plug in to your favourite iTunes. Your child needs interaction and play. Few of us have not made use of the relief that the TV can offer, and how it makes it possible for us to get on with other essential tasks. But you can also sometimes be with your child and share that experience. Be aware that too much of the electronic baby-sitter will have its effect on their development and on your long-term depth of relationship. Disengaged professional child-care can do the same.

So how do you know what to do, at this stage? I want to offer a simple guideline. Let the child tell you. I own up to having been very bad at this and it may push every button you possess of control, ambition and belief that there is a right way. Other parents may trigger thoughts of competition, telling you how their infant is already out of diapers and doing trigonometry. Your fears that your child is less (.......fill in the blank) than they should be could leap out of the cupboard and attack you. Breathe deeply, and trust. Trust yourself, and trust your child. They will develop at their own pace.

How does the child tell you? When you are offering something she wants, she will be happy, absorbed and engaged. At this stage all learning is through play and curiosity. Children will take their world and re-imagine it. They will use sticks or plastic animals to create worlds. They can learn the rudiments of counting, but only through rhymes and games. You can introduce the alphabet, or simple words, but only as play.

Don't test, don't assess. They are never "wrong", and "right" will come with time, familiarity and repetition. "When the fun stops - STOP". Pushing damages their bond with you because even subtle disapproval or disappointment at their performance reduces the feeling of safety. It also

> **Contact is more important than content**

sets up tension and shuts down assimilation. This can affect their future capacity to learn.

The same need to allow him to be who he is applies to behaviour, and many parents find this very difficult. Our world is often not child-friendly. The supermarket looks to them like a great playground full of interesting stuff, just when you have a job to do and a schedule to meet. For the toddler there is this lovely, open, flat space in which to practice walking or running. There is a different acoustic to find how different their voice can sound.

There are LOTS of attractive THINGS to be curious about, in bright and colourful packets. They want the toilet at the most inconvenient time, are screaming with teething pains in the most embarrassing way. Society thinks that you should be in control. Don't take it on board – they only think that because their own Purple stage was badly handled. You only feel bad because you too have been programmed with unreasonable expectations. Smile at the disapproval as if you are too dim to know better. Breathe Deeply, Trust and Be Patient.

During this stage, your child is never being naughty. This may be hard to grasp because it is an unfamiliar point of view and it will change with the next stage. Please try not to dismiss it and don't mistake where I am going with it. I am not saying that children should be allowed to run riot. But they cannot manage their curiosity and desire to experiment, so you have to manage them. At this age they can't understand punishment in relation to specific behaviour, and all punishment will do is make them feel threatened and unsafe. They cannot understand reasons.

Even if they seem to have enough language they have no logical brain capacity because that physiology has not developed yet. So attempting to explain has nowhere to land in their system. It is a waste of your time. It frustrates you and only confuses them. All of this means that you have to learn how to lead. They don't know how to be other than they are. The most you can do is distract or divert. If you have an agenda, make them a part of it. Stop them if it is dangerous. Contain them if that is necessary, for example putting them in the child seat and be prepared to put up with the crying.

Just last weekend I was at a café in a public space connected with a historic building. A mixed environment with mature couples, singles, young couples and families of all kinds.

At one table was a couple, thirties-ish with their two-year-old girl. She was drinking water from a light disposable cup, through a straw, and the cup tipped over. Water went over the table, chair and child's clothes.

If they hadn't been in my sightline, I would not have known anything had happened. There was no shocked exclamation, no cross word at the child, no criticism of her mistake. The girl didn't cry. "Did your water fall over?" was all that was said. No drama, no fuss.

Calmly mum raised the girl on to her lap and held her there. Dad went for napkins. Mum took off the girl's clothes and replaced them with dry ones from the bag they had with them. Dad wiped table, chair and floor. After a short while the little girl was back on her chair with a new, not very full cup, blowing bubbles in the water through her straw.

How do you feel when you read this story? Would you have behaved like that? Would you like to, or do you think that the little girl will grow up more careless, for not being chastised? I suggest that this story is a recipe for low stress and happy holidays.

There is one more BIG consequence of how the Purple system works in the child. I have said that it is imitative. This means that a child is learning through watching what you do, listening to what you say, copying and repeating it back. Remember you are Chief – a status next to Godhead. They will do what you do and speak as you speak. So the big rule is:-

***Don't do or say anything that you would not want them to replay in front of their teacher / the minister and congregation / your mother / the queue at the checkout.***

Children at this stage are incapable of working with "Do as I say, not as I do". That mechanism has not been built yet.

I repeat; you cannot explain or rationalise your decisions. Little by little, cause and effect is learned by experience. It is what toddlers do. So don't explain that the sharp knife is dangerous. Just calmly remove it.

If learning by experience will not bring serious harm you may want to warn them "If you do that it will hurt" and allow them to get the lesson if they don't listen, because that way the lesson will truly be taken on board. This is against the grain of our "Health and Safety" culture. You will have to be the judge of course, but preventing children from having unpleasant experiences risks them growing up unnecessarily fearful and lacking in resilience. They don't learn to cope with adversity.

Lastly, if you want a child in the Purple stage to do something different than they are doing now, don't forbid them or tell them why they must stop. Take them gently by the hand and lead them towards an alternative. Show them the way.

## Red: Parent as Border Patrol

I once heard this definition of the stages in infancy.

1. Pre-crawl.
2. Crawling.
3. Walking.
4. Out of Control

Welcome to the Red stage in human development.

I have avoided putting time-lines on Beige and Purple. Children differ, stages overlap, and it is in the nature of the spiral that each stage includes the previous ones. Beige and Purple are our foundations; we don't stop being concerned with our personal survival and we never quite let go of Father Christmas. Even if we reject them, our parents live in us all our lives. But if you have heard of or experienced the "terrible two's", you have a fair notion of when Red starts. With most children, you'll know for sure when it kicks in. There are reasons too, why you should welcome it.

In the spiral of human development, there is an oscillation between stages that are collective and others that are individualistic. Tribal Purple is strongly collective. But the life conditions that it creates can be limiting. Ancestral wisdom can fail to meet changing circumstances. New energies need to assert themselves. There is a healthy impulse for those with initiative and drive to explore creative and expansive options, which may take them out of the tribal agreement. The downside of this impulse is that it can be over-assertive. The individual "power to" can become "power over". Historically this developed tribal warlords; in a modern context it shows up in thug-led street gangs and mafia bosses.

For the developing infant it is essential and healthy that they begin to chart their course away from being the same as mom and dad, and start to find out who they are. They need to develop their sense of "I". This is often a strong life-force, **assertive and impulsive**. They feel the force of their own desires and emotions in an impulsive and raw way. "I want what I want and I want it NOW".

A child at this stage will begin to say "no". Depending on their nature, this can go into full-scale resistance and tantrums where they lay kicking and screaming on the floor. There are several stages in child-rearing where the need for love is greatest exactly when you may feel it is least deserved. This is one of them.

Your child still has no ability to rationalise. You cannot persuade him out of a tantrum. However hard you try to tell him the reasons why, he cannot hear them. You can't make this happen faster so my advice remains - don't waste your breath. Generally you can't stop the emotion either. He will have to express his anger until it is spent, and trying to prevent this is very hard work. Distraction may work, but it is by no means certain to. Put him gently where he can't hurt himself or damage other people and things and

> One colleague of mine had a child who when in a tantrum would hold his breath. He would do this until he turned blue. Nothing would stop him. Eventually he and his wife learned that it is physiologically impossible to kill yourself this way. The breathing reflex will always kick in. Of course, that was very scary at the time. I tell this story only to let you know just how much determination is present, and how much patience you might need.

let him get on with it. I even knew one parent who would join in – lying on the floor and screaming. This was apparently very effective if you are inclined to try it. Though I would suggest the opposite of the TV demonstration advice – i.e. "don't try this outside the home." Unless you are really brave, of course. Or have a very theatrical streak and a sense of humour. You might like to imagine it though.

From the child's point of view, learning "who am I" and experiencing "what do I feel" involves testing themselves against the world. They have to gain the inner experience of consequences and they have no other way to do this. In Purple they had no boundaries, and (ideally) that has been safe because those around would meet their needs. Understanding "who I am" calls for an experience of "who others are". There is insecurity underneath this separation. Your job at this stage is to provide the boundaries. It is a very important job – one of the most important you will ever perform. Siblings too will often provide instant and visceral feedback. This may need managing to prevent extremes, but not to prevent the learning that is available.

To do all of this, you will need to know your own boundaries. One of the reasons that we all struggle with this is that few of us had a completely satisfactory Red stage ourselves. And even if we did, we all have days when we are very clear, and others when we are not. Your child cannot help but challenge this. DON'T TAKE IT PERSONALLY! The only constructive and effective choice you have is to get clear what **your** boundaries are and then hold them as firmly but lovingly as you know how.

> **It's not about you.
> Don't take it
> personally.**

Understand that when I say "your" boundaries, I am not just talking about your likes and dislikes. They also include your judgement about what is good for the child. What time they should go to bed; how many sweets they are allowed; what they may or may not watch on TV; all of these amount to your boundaries. Make a decision, tell your child firmly what that is and STICK TO IT. You cannot negotiate with the Red stage. You may get tears, anger, sulks or tantrums. There is nothing that you can do about that except be patient, and when emotions are a bit calmer, lead them or distract them into something else.

## This is not an opportunity for negotiation

Recognise too that few of these decisions are permanent. Bedtime will be a continuous negotiation - probably until you are going to bed before them. TV rules will change with age. With more than one child, you will have to make decisions that work for two or more. Those decisions will never be fair – they can't be. It is OK that they aren't fair. We all know that life is never guaranteed to be completely fair as we ourselves see it, and your child will have to come to terms with the fact that you are doing the best that you can. But almost all rules change with age, or with what the child is ready for. There is no one right answer and that is good, because that way you can't get it wrong, and you are allowed to change.

The holding of boundaries is important for a number of reasons. When you remember that your child is giving up their Purple form of security for this new experience, recognise that it is very scary not to encounter any boundaries at all. However much she may protest at the boundary you have just set, there is also a security for her in knowing that she is still held. Your "no" may seem as if it hurts, but it can be the most loving word of all. So try to deliver it with love! However many times you have to repeat it.

> **"No" can be the most loving word. Deliver it with love**

Another reason why it is important is that she is learning – not in an intellectual sense but as a very gut-level experience – that she is not omnipotent. Learning who she is, also means to learn that she is not the whole universe. However obvious that may seem to you, for her it is not. She finds that her "I" is encountering others who also have an "I". There is a journey from the compliance that comes with early dependency, toward co-operation. It is a journey that will ebb and flow over the years.

Red is impulsive. It is driven by desire and appetite. The inner seeking for his own power shows itself as a battle for power over others. He has no guilt, because there are no internalised rules and that neurology hasn't been built yet, but there can be some shame. This does not have to be – should not be – a big thing. You want to impose a boundary but not to destroy his will – not if you want him to have the inner strength later in life to achieve his goals. But the "time out" or "naughty step" can be quite

> Useless question
> 
> "Why did you do that?"

shaming enough. It is OK that he sits there until he is ready to say "sorry". And he should be hugged and even praised for saying sorry, whether he meant it or just did it to appease. He needs to feel the separation that comes with offending others and he needs to experience the love and forgiveness that comes with acceptance. The shame must not be permanent. This is an obvious Christian message for those who know the parable of the prodigal son, but it is also a universal truth. Without the possibility of redemption, we are all lost. As parents, we must learn to forgive quickly.

If, as is traditional, there are two parents, you will have to agree what your rules are. Children are unbelievably skilled at spotting discrepancies between daddy's boundaries and mummy's. They notice things even if they can't yet reason, and even when language is limited Red is naturally cunning. If they get a "no" from one and a "yes" from the other they will exploit that. Sometimes it will be OK for you to have different boundaries in small things. But most of the time it is more supportive to the child to have consistency. And it is very important not to have one of you consistently be "the nice one". With any couple, there will often be times where one is holding the line strongly, and another feels to cut a little slack. We all have grumpy days. But share those roles. It is OK for your child to see that people are individuals, and not totally consistent (just as was the case with not being totally fair) but learning to manipulate his parents is not so good. Single parents may escape this problem, but may on the other hand lack someone to back them up when it is tough, and consistency becomes a matter of stamina under pressure.

The Red stage is very precious. It can be hard because it pokes the places in our own unconscious where we stored memories of not getting what we wanted, of being crushed, of being over-harshly parented. We may have to look at why we are being rigid. Equally we may have to examine why we cannot hold to a decision, and why their expression of upset triggers our own buried hurts. I am not saying that we all have to go into psychotherapy. But you are a grown-up. You have learned to manage your own Red. Your child may simply be giving you an opportunity to refine that ability.

## Blue: Parent as Rule-maker

In the big Spiral picture, Red is a very long-lived stage. It is still present on the planet in the many warlord cultures, like Somalia or parts of Afghanistan. But it has limitations. Power struggles result in continuous instability. Warlords who age may become interested in a lasting legacy, in knowing whether there is a higher purpose, or in something that secures them (and often their family too) against the next pretender to their throne. In addition, as societies become larger, more settled, and with more complex needs, systems of order are needed. This calls for **codes to live by**, structures that outlast individuals, secure means of trade and codes that keep neighbours at peace. The Blue stage coincides with written rules, legal codes and police enforcement, religious systems and priesthoods (judaeo-christian, islamic), accounting and trading governance.

So it is with childhood. As the infant emerges from the turbulence of the Red years, it begins to re-awaken its curiosity about the collective. It is another swing from being about "I" toward questions of how "we" live together. Individual boundaries are not enough and there are containers for "my will". Her family is surrounded by something bigger. She may not have a concept for what society is, but she knows it is there.

Blue begins to emerge out of Red as the child develops a kind of pattern-recognition about the ways in which her impulses are responded to. This is a very gradual process, but over a long period she becomes socialised and accepts that there are generic codes about not taking someone else's toy, about not hitting, about one cookie each. The fairness of one cookie each may have been present from early on as an instinctive knowing. The codes are now being made more explicit, turning into rules.

Blue development is a long stage. It is beginning to be visible at the end of kindergarten and will last all the way to pre-puberty. All development is underpinned by changes in the body and brain. Some children take a long time to develop bladder control to full overnight dryness. They may relapse under stress. Usually there will be accidents before this mechanism is secure. And so it is with the management of the Red impulsivity. It will continue to break through. Blue has some understanding of consequences, but the early phase of Blue may not be good at articulating this or at self-managing. Obviously, children will vary.

Blue likes rules, and will become more attentive to consistency, and to the need for reliable application. And as Blue develops, there will be the beginnings of a wish to have explanations. Why is this decision different from that one? We all know that there is comfort to be derived from knowing just where one stands. When we know what is right, we do not have to face the shame of getting it wrong. For the child, that shame of how others are seeing them is gradually internalised as guilt.

> **In Praise of praise.** Maybe it reflects the 10 commandments that we think so much about what you must not do. One effect of that seems to be that we let our children do what they want and only have anything to say when they need correction. I encourage you to think about doing something different. Imagine that you are sitting in a cafe where you need your child to be quiet and considerate of others. What if you were to regularly praise him for doing well, rewarding him with your approval and recognising his success?

In Disney's Pinocchio, Jiminy Cricket sings "always let your conscience be your guide". This message is of no use to Red, but the Blue child is developing a conscience, moving from "what do I want to do" towards "what is the right thing to do". Blue is about **codes to live by** and children grasp that. Most of them want it, though not in excess and not in a punitive way.

There is challenge in writing about this stage at it onset because the early stage of Blue looks more grown-up than it is. Later on (Rudolf Steiner saw this as coming with the second teeth) there is development of a new kind of learning. But for a long time the magical thinking of the Purple stage continues to be present all the way through Red and early Blue. We do not have to understand Spiral theory to know this. The child at six is often not ready to know that Father Christmas is make-believe and we protect him instinctively. Up until this age, learning is primarily through imagination and play and many children will respond poorly to formal education or to too much formal instruction, too soon.

# More Brainwaves

From approximately age 2, up to 5 or six, the child develops slightly higher brain wave patterns. These are still not adult-like, but are more awake than the Delta state of 0-2.

These **Theta waves** measure 4 to 8 cycles per second. This continues to be an abstract and imagination-led world and the child may be connected to their internal world, or even trance-like. Critical, rational thinking is still foreign to them, particularly in the Red stage. The transitions being described here are gradual and there is no neat cut-off.

Children will accept what you tell them, except when it conflicts with their impulses. So if you offer them rules or definitions or supposed truths "boys are smarter than girls", "your sister is prettier than you", "you'll never amount to anything"; these statements may go in deep, especially with repetition. Language and linguistic memory are now well established. The Theta brain-waves are higher than the unconscious of Delta. What happens now is more in the realm of the subconscious, which is why such early programs are powerful. As the Jesuits said, give me the child until he is seven and I will show you the man.

Between five and eight, even while the Blue stage is still very much in development, brain waves change further to the **Alpha** frequencies of 8 to 13 cycles per second. Only now does the analytical mind begin to form properly, and this is how children are able to interpret and embed more formal constructs regarding the laws of external life. However, the imaginary world is still present, and children will continue to be good at pretending. They are straddling the earlier and newer realities.

> Alpha is the target level of brainwaves for many forms of meditation in adults, as we seek to slow down and engage with our subconscious and, in some systems, tap into our inner world. In this we are re-opening the door between subconscious and conscious minds, and synchronising our brain hemispheres. That door had gradually closed between ages 8 and 12.

Potentially a challenge arises here because in describing the liking for rules, it may seem as if I am encouraging an engagement with the child's mind. At the start of Blue, this is not as helpful as it looks to be. It pulls the child into intellect before he is ready, when his brain structures are not present to handle it. He may well try to simulate the understanding, but this may be at the expense of flexibility in thinking. This imbalance may make creative problem-solving more difficult, and undermine the Orange stage that is to come.

One of the ways that the Red-Blue child can engage with this is through regularity and rhythm. When days have a pattern, when weeks are similar and when the seasons are recognised, this builds a platform of stability and security that is non-verbal and non-intellectual. For many of us as parents this is not easy – there are so many pressures on our time and external demands on our schedules that it is hard to create regularity and family routine. I don't want to add to the stresses of modern existence. But often having a focus on this question enables us to find anchor points.

While on the subject of pressure, it is a general truth that modern life is not child-friendly. A visit to a supermarket or mall can become a nightmare and is the most frequent place that I witness unpleasant treatment of children by harassed parents. Some cultures are more tolerant than others, and in those which are not child-friendly it is important to develop a thick skin against disapproval when children are merely being noisy or playful. Often though, the stress comes from the parent's challenge to complete the shopping task quickly. It helps if we can relax about that.

When a child is in the Blue stage, parental influence is one among many. They are receiving guidance from school, increasingly from other parents or "activity" clubs and leaders. Engagement in team sports builds a healthy balance of Red and Blue, calling for the individual heroism within a collective purpose. Music can develop similar structures. An 8 to 15-year-old who has not yet learned internal control of their Red may be an ideal candidate for a martial arts training, which will call forth internal discipline, and will often be taught by someone who can embody a form of centred authority which will draw more respect than many of us can manage as parents.

I described Blue as the stage in the big picture where religious structures, codes and priesthoods arise. Our laws may echo the "thou shalt nots" of the commandments in ways which even the non-religious would not question. But religions vary hugely. We are accustomed to refer to Christians in a collective way, when the underlying truth is that there are wide variations from fundamentalist to free-thinking. In fact, a fundamentalist Christian may have more in common with a fundamentalist Jew or Muslim than any of these do with their more liberal and reforming sub-groups.

It would be wrong for me to prescribe attitudes and choices here, as well as potentially offensive and unlikely to be listened to by those of strong faith. But I would like to say something about the balances that are present, and about the potential consequences of some choices.

It is well-known that the Jesuits said "give me the child until he is seven and I will show you the man". For many, the establishment of habits and rhythms is embedded both in the family or ancestral Purple and in the surrounding culture. This can provide a core strength. I rather like a statement from Cindy Wigglesworth[2], to the effect that *"Rituals exist for us – they are not there to please God."* There is comfort in this form of order. And in days past, when the culture as a whole was strongly inhabited by a Blue order, the children would grow up with a set of Values that matched their life conditions.

> **Rituals exist for us....**
> **They're not there to please God**

In the North Americas and in Europe, our general culture is deeply in the next, Orange stage, and with significant amounts of the Green Values system present or rising (details follow shortly). We have all seen plays, films or TV dramas in which an authoritarian parent meets with the consequences of children who are moving away from the traditions and the rules. The musical "Fiddler on the Roof" exemplifies this, as Tevye

---

[2] Developer of the Deep Change SQ21 system for Spiritual Intelligence development

comes to terms with his four daughters as they find other things more important than the tradition, or even the Faith.

When they eventually reach adulthood your child will need to be equipped to function well in a complex and diverse world. This does not mean that they cannot hold on to their core principles, but there is more demand than ever to live with and thrive amidst diversity. We will also see as we examine the Orange stage that it is necessary and healthy for children to re-examine what they have been given, and to choose for themselves.

At every stage of development, parents steer a course on one side of which is too much structure – a rigidity which can undermine self-confidence, sap willpower and suppress creativity. We all know of the bullying macho father who puts so much pressure on his son to be tough and to be a man that he ends up fulfilling his worst fears by producing a son who disappoints and who possibly also has to get away, living in distant fear and hatred.

Dramas thrive on these scenarios. There are some sons who will survive this treatment and develop the strength to meet father's demands, but they may then behave just like him. Sometimes, bullies breed bullies. One very good friend put up with the treatment until he was 15, then knocked his father cold. He became a strong man who in his sixties won a medal for bravery rescuing a child from drowning, almost dying himself. He is also a recovering alcoholic who for many years was abusive.

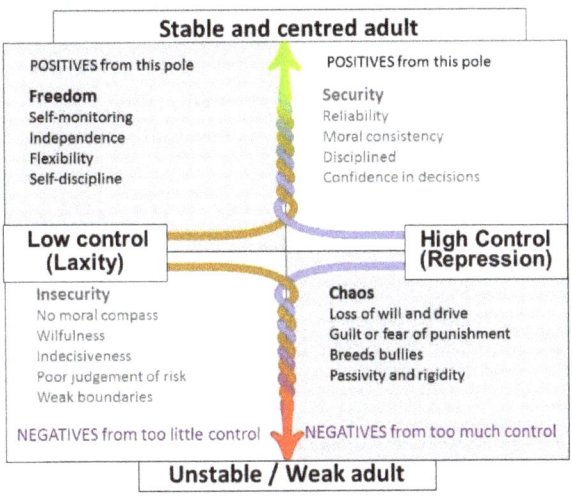

*With acknowledgements to Barry Johnson "Polarity Management"*

On the other side from abuse is the danger of too little structure, of weak boundaries and lack of guidance. Whether a parent lacks strength, does not believe they have the right, or thinks that letting everything go is being kind and loving, the child grows up rudderless. They have nothing to guide them and nothing even to rebel against. Inside they may forever feel abandoned, and find it harder to stand up for themselves against others. Some children will find their own path, often by latching onto someone or something outside the home that provides the stability they need. Some will be lost. Those who fail to develop internal structure may be the most likely to take foolish risks later with drugs, to be coerced into sex or unable to find a sense of personal direction.

As a parent you have more than a right to provide guidelines. In my view you have a duty. Your child's success depends on it. Sometimes tough love is the best kind. But it cannot be the only kind. Tough love works best when it is embedded in warmth, care and kindness, balanced with approval and recognition. Give your child the benefit of your wisdom and also allow them to develop their own.

You have a long time in which to practice this skill and also a long time in which to redress any imbalances. It's a very forgiving process. If you are an established parent reading any of this, and thinking that you could have done some things better, it is rarely too late to rebalance.

I should also say at this point that if you think what I am saying is nonsense that is OK too. Spiral Dynamics is a theory. It is not an "ism" that prescribes what is right. It is a tool for reflection and a fresh way to view important parts of our lives. It is your choice.

Blue is an extended stage during which your child will be developing all the time, growing in understanding, learning by doing, learning from their peers, still mixing play-learning with absorption of lessons from teachers, books, movies, and peer-groups. Child Blue understands reasoning and likes it, but is not yet skilled in analysis – a skill which is yet to develop and may not come into play at all. There are many people in the world who will live their lives with apparent success without any need for it.

Such individuals find their place in the system where they know what the rules require of them and are content to work within the constraints. They may be the ones who believe that the rewards come in another life. They may be the ones who find their bliss in the simple pleasures like creating stable and loving relationships, or in their hobbies and interests. It is quite possible to thrive into old age with Blue values, particularly if the conditions they live in are stable. It is no failure to bring up a child who is happy with their lot.

As we engage in this narrative with the stages yet to come, be aware that while Western culture has moved very strongly into them and thus sets widely shared expectations for achievement and perceived success, these are still choices. You don't have to judge yourself or your child by them and it may be healthiest if you do not.

## Orange: Parent as Manager

In the socio-historical development of humanity, Orange is a relatively recent stage, and it is one which many countries of the world have not yet fully acquired. For example, China is emerging into it, but even now has a mix of Blue communist system culture and roots in a traditional, quite Purple Confucianism with its deep respect for elders and ancestors. Most of Africa lives with a mix of Purple, Red and Blue life conditions and values.

The conditions which call forth Orange ways of thinking are formed in the limitations that Blue Values bring. This is a swing from the orderly Values of collective rules into the next stage of individualistic assertion. But where Red assertion mixed heroism with self-gratification and power-seeking, Orange individuality has Blue under its belt. Orange feels the Blue rules restricting its inventiveness, creativity and ability to bring forth the new. But it has also learned the rules.

Like Red, Orange human aspires to a better life for himself, but where Red would look for dominance, Orange is more **strategic**. A Red-embedded human doesn't recognise rules as such, only the power of those who enforce them. They don't exist for her. Orange knows the rules are there, but seeks to bend them, change them or failing that, to avoid being caught. Blue rules feel like a restriction and sometimes they are, as with Russian communism which controlled to death what, given the strengths of their educational system, might otherwise have been a successful economy.

The great positive value of Orange in human development is that it is an **inventive, creative surge**. In our history it brought science, the development of navigation that opened the new world and the rise of technology through the industrial revolution as well as cheap fossil-fuel energy to power the machines. The expansion of America and the rise of Orange came hand in glove. Orange creates material prosperity and surplus. Today's leisure rests on Orange labour-saving devices, and welfare systems, healthcare and pensions are supported by its surplus wealth.

So how does this relate to the development of your child?  Let's talk first about an idealised scenario.  A child who has experienced balanced Red, Purple and Blue arrives at her teens ready to find out **for herself** who she truly is, and what she is here to do.  True intellectual capability is only now kicking in and will take years to mature.  The brain processes which allow deep enquiry cause the teenager to question everything, and nothing is sacred.  The first thing that the teenager needs to invent is herself.

In order to do this she must distance herself from her parents.  She will become focussed on her peer group, or on subsets of that group, possibly trying out a succession of identities in a compare and contrast exercise.  She will seek her security with those peers and appear to want as little contact with parents as possible.  Some of the search is generational, as a whole cohort of youth begins to set the agenda for their adulthood.  Nature supports the process by creating surges of hormones that break down previously established order in the brain and body-mind.  Depending on temperament, this may bring out varying amounts of conflict and rebellion.

I have described that ideal from imagination because I have not witnessed it and it's my guess is that it doesn't ever quite happen like that.  The teenage years are an opportunity for parents to experience one of nature's mixed blessings.  It gives you and your child the opportunity to fix anything that has been left undone in the establishment of Red stage capacities.  What happens in practice is a kind of deep Orange, some parts of it indistinguishable from Red.  This is the ugly face of teenage-hood.  How deep it gets may depend a little on how successfully Red was handled – in case you need an extra incentive to make an effort then!  Now more than ever we can apply the observation that the greatest love is needed at times when it seems least deserved, least invited, least received and least rewarded.  If we can hang in there, the eventual rewards are huge, both in their flourishing and in the richness of the relationship that is possible.

> **Love is needed most..**
>
> **when it seems least deserved, least invited, least received and least rewarded**
>
> *Believed based on Swedish Proverb*

The same boundary-setting task will be required now as in the infant stage. They are different boundaries, but just as necessary. The same tensions will be present for the young adult. That is, they will want the security of knowing that you care, but may rather die than admit or show that. They will want total independence at the same time as your continued support for all their wants. Red impulsiveness will be present again, compounded by hormonal swings. Remember that you have been there too, and consider whether some retrospective sympathy for your parents may be warranted. ☺

In Red, I suggested that you avoid rationalisation, whereas teenagers will insist that you justify your actions and will have some very interesting logic to apply to how wrong you are. Listen carefully, because they may know something that you don't. The Red part of this battle will be about power, and there may be some implied threats. The Orange part will be more manipulative, and almost any trick is seen as legitimate to someone deeply in this Values system.

There are only two containers for this aspect of Orange. One is the presence of robust Blue rules and enforcement, absence of which allows the family equivalents of Enron; which is to say that you will be royally screwed. So as a parent you need to maintain strong Blue structures, finding the right balance of strength and fairness. This can be a challenge for some of us. It may bring up our own unresolved teenage upsets. Alternatively it may be because our own Values systems are not strong in Blue, and we may also not be oriented to the collective thinking of the other "cool-colour" systems, Purple and Green.

Some of us are more centred in the warm colour (Red/Orange) individualistic Values systems. The difficulty with this is that it becomes a very personal trial of strength, based on what we each want. If you recognise the value of the Blue system, you have the backing of something besides your own opinion and wishes.

The other container often cannot come until later, and that is to help your teen develop self-moderation through the Green Values system. That may be more appealing to many adults who themselves have strong Green Values. But as we will see shortly, Green can be averse to the use of Blue rules and wish to be tolerant and permissive. If you are not willing to invoke the Blue system, you risk failing to give your child the safe base that they need and you may deprive yourself of any control over what happens. The challenge provided by the teenager in Orange is another opportunity for us to learn about ourselves. It's a management training course!

As stated above, teenagers will tend to withdraw. This can present an array of difficult emotional scenarios. Mothers who have been close to their sons, and fathers to their daughters can find this time very uncomfortable, though the distancing will usually happen with both parents. It brings up our feelings of rejection, and if not that, simple grief at the loss of closeness. If you handle this well, there will be a reward 5-10 years later, because your child will come back as a potential friend for life. <u>However personal this rejection looks, it is not about you</u>. For mothers and sons, this is also the stage when he needs one or more strong male role models. This doesn't have to be father, though it's great when that happens. Teachers, sports coaches, ministers, grandfathers can provide this too – it doesn't matter where it comes from. But he has to let go of the apron strings and find out what it is to be a man. Very rarely can mothers do this. There is an equivalent of this for girls, who need female role models. Lone parents may need to actively seek the necessary support.

It is in any case a good idea for you to encourage your child to have connection with other adults. Of course you need to know they are trustworthy but you don't need them to be people who will agree with you, only that they are people who will be there for your child to turn to when they cannot or will not turn to you. There was a time when godparents fulfilled that function, and sometimes uncles, aunts and grandparents will do this. But sometimes it helps if the person is not so close to the family. Someone perceived as a trusted outsider may be the one they are able to go to.

For both genders it is hard, even in these days of sexual openness, for all subjects to be open. The ease with which the physical aspects can be talked of, and the wealth of information that children will get through the web, magazines and TV creates an illusion that everything is sorted. Not so. Behind that are all the anxieties about body image, complex and turbulent feelings; the pressure to have a boy / girlfriend; the insecurity and self-doubt when they don't. Understanding the risks of STD's, the emotional consequences of deciding to have sex, the risks of getting drunk and embarrassingly photo-tagged on Facebook, together with the challenges of effective contraception present a nightmare to parents at a time when communication is at its most limited.

This makes many parents insecure. You are not in control. You may want to be, and may lay down all sorts of rules to make yourself feel better, but you can't control this. Remember how you got round your parents. Think of all the things that you did that they still don't know about. In my experience you can only guide, and manage the risks as much as possible.

Personally I recommend talking about these issues very early – in the pre-teen and early teen years. Your sons and daughters will need to have some internal strength to guide their own decisions. The better you have managed infant Red and developed robust Blue, the more they will be able to resist pressure, control their impulses and manage their own choices. Now is when you reap the rewards of your earlier attention. Talking openly, at the age when they are still listening, about what is was like when you got really sick-drunk, or how you wish you had waited, or how you felt as a teenager can help a lot. It needs to come up naturally though, by watching for your opportunity. If you push, the door will close.

What I am saying here is that you have to meet their strategic Orange with your own. You need to be canny. You will see things about them that they won't know that you can see. You can anticipate aspects of their lives that are inevitable, and detect when they happen. Use this knowledge and insight for their benefit. In addition, use your knowledge of the world. It is normal for parents to assume that their children will be heterosexual. Remember that they may not be, or that they may go through a period of confusion and uncertainty. Be ready in yourself to handle this.

My favourite expert on emotional and spiritual intelligence, Cindy Wigglesworth, once told me how happy she was when her teenage daughter kept changing her hair colour and style. She was really pleased that the rebellion and challenge was coming out where she could see it, and held her tongue rather than risk causing more covert responses. I see this as great guidance.

It is typical for young people to explore their identity by adopting the styles of several different groups in turn, often in a very random-looking manner, try not to worry about what is happening. Most of the extremes won't last. You don't have to like what you see. You don't have to pretend that you like it. But there is much to be said for tolerating anything which is not obviously damaging to them or others. And even if some styles seem to last a distressingly long time, nearly all of us emerge into the light eventually, and find a functional place in the world. It may feel hard to let them find themselves, but it is a major foundation for a healthy and happy life. That is generally the result that we want, isn't it?

> When my son was 15, I was responsible for giving relationships and sex education to the class he was in. I told them that statistics predicted that one or two of them would be gay. I had no idea that he would be the one. Despite our openness it took him several years to "come out" to us. We suspected it for a long time, and eventually he said "he was waiting for us to ask".

# Final Brainwaves

After the age of eight, brain activity increases to even higher frequencies and above 13 cycles, we reach the category of beta waves. They go up and up, possibly as high as 50cps. Typically in teenage they move from the low to mid-range. This represents the onset and increasing dominance of conscious, analytical thinking. The earlier brainwaves are still present, but overwhelmed. This rise in frequency is the pattern for the Orange stage and beyond. See chart on following page.

Our culture pushes children to become analytical sooner than has historically shown to be natural. This may well be at the expense of their emotional roots, embodied self-awareness and stability, and responsible for some of the challenges that modern teenagers experience. In the push to raise achievers, you may wish to be aware that such early pressure can be counter-productive, and to look at the evidence for emotional intelligence as a primary requirement for career success.

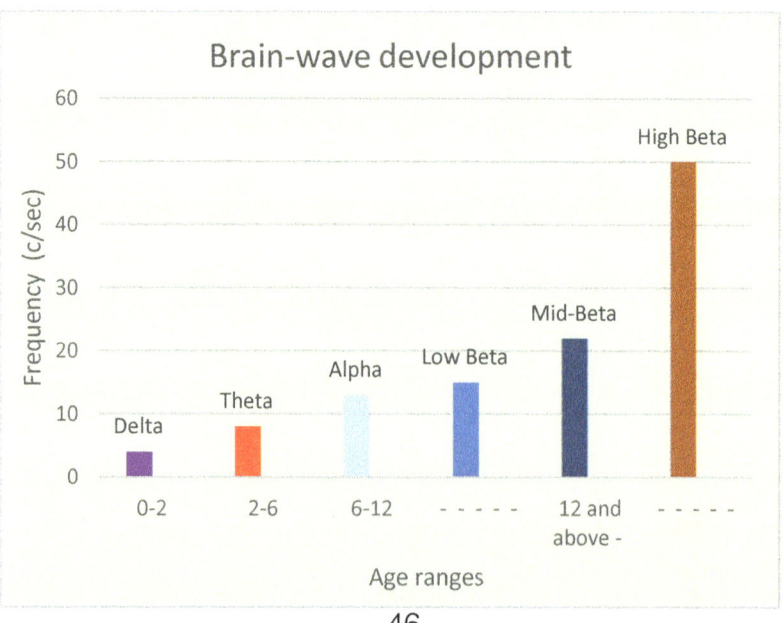

> I have tried to keep these panels oriented to scientific fact. But this is my opinion – for what it is worth. I expect that coming years will see an increasing acknowledgement of the evidence that a healthy human (one who begins to integrate all of these worldviews) will retain more of the earlier stages, including the sensory and embodied awareness that was present in Beige and Purple.
>
> This is prefigured already I suggest, in the work of the mindfulness trend, EQ and SQ, Access Consciousness and of health practitioners like Dr. Joe Dispenza. So while the trajectory so far seems to imply that later stages require higher frequencies even more, I am suggesting that this is becoming a problem and that Yellow-and-above adults will revisit, re-awaken and include more of the Theta and Alpha as an essential feature of their integration.

## Green: Parent as Guide and Mentor

The Green Values stage arises out of Orange because of the limitations of that system. These lie in its strong emphasis on the individual and in a general focus on the material, both in the sense of consumer materialism and in the tendency to move away from human care as well as from spiritual realms. Orange science challenges Blue religion and treats it as superstition. Orange organisations turn people into numbers to manage. Orange achievement is measured by corner offices, the cars we drive and the HDTV in our lounge. In Orange, he who dies with the most toys, wins.

Eventually, there are aspects of this thinking that we become uncomfortable with. This is not just about the excesses of greed and financial corruption, though these may be part of our wake-up call. There are also parts of us that feel undernourished and we hunger for more sense of human connection, to care and be cared for, to be part of a fair world and to understand the inner nature of who we are. The Green Values system brings us psychology, self-help books, peace camps, social systems to support the unemployed, elderly, sick or damaged.  Its keynote is in being human, in **bonding**.  Green has experienced that its material satisfaction did not bring happiness or inner peace.  It may not return to religious spirituality, but instead seeks the **human spirit**.

Aspects of this stage are also present in teenage years, and often intermingle with the Orange.  For instance, while some girls are forming bitchy cliques obsessed with fashion there will be others who become strident in their humanitarianism, and extreme in their concerns for fairness and equality.  Their emotional swings may get channelled into great passions for the rights of animals, or the planet itself.

There is also an odd blend of individualistic focus with a deep need for the security of a peer group. The teenager who becomes a true loner is a rarity, and this may sometimes be a cause for close concern.  But most, even though they may be choosing very strong and unfashionable alternatives – the geeks, the Goths, the punks, they will do so in a tight little collective. The ones who are unable to join with the fashionistas, the cheerleaders or the mainstream macho sports grouping find their alternate corners of security.

The egalitarianism strand of Green can be highly disapproving of both Orange and Blue.  The anti-fashion statement of some of these groups is not only a choice not to compete where they cannot win. It is a deliberate refusal to join in with the perceived unfairness and crass materialism, and rejects the competitiveness on principle.  This refusal to compete can also cause Green to appear unmotivated.

Green treasures freedom for all – the right of the individual to be who he or she is. Since Blue is full of "one right way" rules, this aspect of Green will reject Blue. Blue can also be hierarchical when Green wants to be consensual. Blue likes to have someone to give orders; Green prefers to sit in a circle to reach harmonious agreement. Teenagers may not want to conform with you and society, but they are often insecure if they are unable to conform with each other. This is one reason why cyber-bullying can be so devastating. It may appear to an adult that "sticks and stones can break my bones", but at this age and stage, names can hurt a great deal. They can be psychologically crippling. I won't quote the statistics on self-harm or suicide because the numbers aren't important. It is enough of a risk that you need to be watching for it, and willing to get support.

If your offspring calls you a fascist, you have probably encountered some Green amongst the Orange. But the upside of a Green Values presence is that there is an acknowledgement of fairness. You can call on this Value when it is present, to try to understand your point of view and to meet you half way.

In general, I would feel less need to give guidance on Green. If you are seeing a strong presence of Green Values, the worst is probably over from a parenting point of view. This does not mean that Green cannot give you problems. Any Values system can do that, if it becomes excessive. How comfortable you will be may depend a lot your own core Values system. Just as Green disapproves of Orange and Blue, these Values systems may think of Green as naïve, unrealistic, tree-hugging, flaky and undisciplined. They may dismissively label concern and sensitivity over fairness as "snowflake" attitudes.

Some spiritual or religious Blue perspectives might like Green's fairness, but many of the more traditional and hierarchical forms of Blue might think that socialism is setting in, or feel that the old order is threatened. You may also be recognising that these values clashes are just as much present between adults, and in aspects of political life. Strongly Orange-system parents may feel that their Green offspring are unmotivated, underachieving, unambitious and lacking in competitive edge. How you see their behaviour is now very dependent on where you are looking from, on your own priority codes, and not just on theirs.

I could fill several pages with Values conflicts of this kind. I will confine myself to one more aspect, which is the attitude that the later stages take towards Red. Since you, as a parent, are likely to have a centre of gravity in Blue, Orange or Green, you should understand two potential traps in your management of Red. Blue will generally do alright, provided it is not over-authoritarian, and I have written already of the risk that the child's will-power might be crushed.

There are bigger pitfalls for Orange and Green. Orange, as a fellow warm-colour, individualistic system can be over-allowing, and tolerate Red behaviours that it would be healthier to moderate. Green can see the Red child as a potential victim of authority. "Oh, he's just expressing himself. He needs to be who he is". Green may also tolerate behaviour from teenage Red because "he didn't get enough love". This kind of sympathy can be presented as compassion, but it is often about as caring as giving the whisky bottle back to an alcoholic.

> **It's not them, it's YOU**
>
> <u>Your</u> core attitudes will influence how you respond

It's not just them, <u>it's you</u>. When you read about all of these systems and their interactions, Spiral Dynamics can begin to feel very complex. But even though it is a rich and complex theory, remember that you will generally only have to deal with a portion of this material at any time. The two paragraphs above are offered mainly to alert you to the fact that in all of the interactions, <u>your</u> core attitudes will influence how you respond. They will have been influencing how you read this book. Every stage is an opportunity to look at yourself, at how you were parented and to learn from it. But even if you find my views are not closely aligned with your first thoughts, I hope that they will help you take a fresh look at those responses and respond to the call to be not just one parent, but six different ones over the course of twenty years.

The Spiral journey is not finished, but the culmination will come, if it does come, in adulthood. To know what you might be helping to create, read on.

## The Yellow Stage: Entry into Second Tier: Parents as friends

What does it mean to be an adult? When do we become truly grown-up? I suspect that we all know people who have reached their 30's and more, but who are still behaving like children in some part of their lives. There's the successful businessperson who bullies their family. There's the woman who is an excellent mother, but is unable to clean her house. There are the people who can never keep up with their compulsion to spend money and the ones who drink just a bit too habitually or too much. Some even get to lead countries. You may recognise some aspect of this in yourself; indeed, if you don't you either deserve special congratulations or more likely to be asked to look at yourself again. I say this without criticism as I have witnessed it in myself over the decades and I hear it from my coaching clients. It's the human condition, bless us.

And what does it take to create a functioning world in today's conditions? We see corporations that can make profits but which abuse their employees, damage the environment, late-pay their suppliers, bribe their way around regulation. And we see others which are trying their very hardest to do things well and honestly, but which are unable to keep up with all of the demands placed on them, or to cope with the pace and unpredictability of change.

Of course, none of us is a super-human who can do everything brilliantly. We all have our failings. Past sixty, I think I am approaching competence! But what is it that makes for a rounded, effective and generally well-balanced grown-up? The answer I will give as with everything else here is framed in Spiral terms.

Looking at the development of human society, each of the stages we have been through has been associated with increasing numbers of people living in close proximity (though not necessarily closer socially) from tribes, to towns, to cities. Each stage brings more interactions, more technology and more systems, such that our modern world is fast-moving and globalised. A heat-wave in Russia can affect the grain supply and price all around the world. The company you work for may go out of business this year because of an innovation on the other side of the planet.

Societies which are still using Red-Blue Values systems for their decision-making can buy Orange system weaponry to use on their neighbours. Deep Red-value terrorists who see themselves as disempowered, or subject to rules that they do not have allegiance to, can strike at the heart of the developed Orange-system world, as they did on 9/11, and continue in smaller ways to do. In the big picture, our challenge is to harmonise a world in which all of the first six colour systems are living, and often clashing with each other; all are competing, as Spiral pioneer Don Beck would say, for their sound-bite on CNN.

In the first six Values stages, each of earlier stages remains present and accessible to us. When family survival is at stake, even the most law-abiding Blue individual will loot shops, as was witnessed in New Orleans during Hurricane Katrina. The life conditions require Beige survivalist thinking, and there it is, automatically. When attacked in the street at night, you have to make a rapid decision about your Red power status. Are you able to fight and win – to succeed in direct Red-system confrontation? Do you have an alternative strategy? Or is your appropriate Red response to acknowledge that you have less power, hand over your wallet and avoid being stabbed? Or not be out alone in the first place?

But although these thinking systems are available to you, if you are well-embedded in one of them, you are likely to see the downsides of the others, just as entrepreneurial Orange can see Blue rules as rigidly unimaginative and restrictive, and look on Red as using muscle and anger when some smart manipulation would be much more successful. At both individual and societal level, managing the many stresses of a complex life requires something more than this. We need the capacity to see all of the levels and to know what they are good for. We need to know how each of them looks when they are not healthy, and how to come back into balance.

Looked at through the Spiral lens, the culmination of healthy child development is that the emerging seventh-stage adult will have within them a healthy set of stages one through six, and will be using each of the systems as required to meet the individuals and situations that they come into contact with. Each set of Values contains a necessary set of responses to life conditions, available as a toolset for us to use when needed.

Parents never completely stop being parents. Most continue to worry and provide support. Today's economic challenges are keeping children dependent for longer. But your well-developed child will be finding his/her own feet, entering adulthood, potentially forming a relationship, starting a career and even on the way to being a parent themselves. Now you can stop telling them what to do. Now you can become a friend, someone who no longer gives instruction and generally only gives advice when asked. Fire yourself as parent and save them the trouble of firing you. If you have managed all of the previous six stages moderately well, there is a

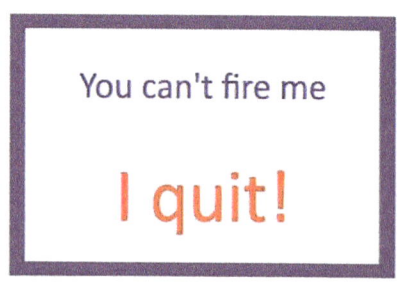

good chance that you will now have a very special friend in your life, a source of continuing pride, joy and even mutual support.

I hope that this journey through the Spiral Dynamics model, and its possible guidance for parents has helped you. And whatever the outcome and whatever the challenges you meet on the way, I hope that you never forget to praise yourself for your successes and for the willingness to give so hugely of yourself as nearly all of us do. It's a hero's journey. May your efforts, your children and you be blessed.

# Postscript 1: A note about time

It may help you to know that the different stages operate on different time-horizons.

Through the first three stages, covering up to the age of 3 and beyond, life is immediate. There is only the now. Although a three-year-old can be told that Father Christmas will come on a special day, this is only conceived of as "not yet, not now". In their present time reality, it is the same as "no". Even telling them that they can have food or drink "When they get home" leaves them in the physiological or psychological tension of not having what they want. They can only be motivated by rewards which are instant. Even adults in Red are like this, and some sports teams in the US learned that to motivate Red-stage individuals, the bonus must be awarded no later than the end of the game. End of season simply does not work for them

A sense of time arises with Blue and it extends year by year. At the start, Blue begins to develop the capacity to defer gratification, but this may be measured in minutes or hours. So they can be motivated by a reward in the future, but to start with can't wait very long. "Be good now and you can watch TV when we get home". Little by little this time extends, so knowing there is pocket-money at the end of the week becomes a realistic target. Longer-term rewards are effective later on, and as adults those in the Blue stage can believe that the reward for virtue comes in heaven.

# Postscript 2: Teaching children about choices

It is very probable that you were raised and educated, just as I was, to believe that choices are made on the basis of right and wrong. You may choose to dismiss what I am about to say because it may seem very different and unfamiliar. However, I feel it is important to make you aware of this perspective and encourage you to give it some consideration.

Life is increasingly complex and unpredictable. The choices of what to do are becoming less and less clear.

It can seem as if right and wrong are moral choices, and in some cases they are. Stealing might be a simple example of "always wrong". It's a Commandment, after all, and yet I gave an example earlier of how the typically religious folk of New Orleans turned to looting during Hurricane Katrina when their lives and those of their children depended on it.

For the future, and for their life in an increasingly complex world, children will need a different kind of skill in their decision-making. This is already a reality since working with others in collaborative ways already means that they have to flex and take into account the needs of others while remaining true to themselves. Rarely are there simple tick-box responses.

So how do children learn to choose? The answer is that they have to gain skill in recognizing the effect of their choices. They need to be asking "what will this create in my life?" and learning how to sense what that outcome might be. Along with the predetermined right-wrong simplicity, we have also been trained and educated in cause-and-effect thinking. Often that seems to call for analysis and factual knowledge. It still implies that there is a right answer, if you can figure it out.

When the world is complex, when other people are involved, when unpredictability is becoming the only certainty, analysis doesn't cut it because there is not enough information or time to think it through. Such a world demands a greater intuitive awareness, an ability to sense what cannot be computed.

If that seems fanciful or bordering mystical, I encourage you to see it as more normal than that. A soccer player is not analyzing the game. They are aware of the movement of their team-mates and their opponents. They know where the ball is. The best players have an instinctive ability to sense the patterns and to know where the ball will be. They have built their awareness through experience and practice. The game itself is always asking questions of them and they are making choices all the time.

Another image that I use often is that of a surfer riding a big wave. You can't analyse the wave. You can't surf by being on the beach, calculating. A wave has a life all of its own and each one is unique. The surfer is feeling their body position, the balance of the board, the movements of the wind and the water, responding in millisecond increments to avoid wipe-out. The assessment they are making is not "what is right or wrong?" Rather it is, at a very physical level, a rapid assessment of "what will this choice create?" and they remake that assessment continuously.

What if we were to retrain ourselves, and encourage our children to live in their own continuous assessment, develop for themselves an ever-present awareness of what their choice will create?

In the early stages that may mean that you tell them. When you see them about to touch the candle flame, the simplest response is to say "Don't". But if instead you say "if you do that, it will hurt", you create a new frame for them, even though they are not sensing the outcome for themselves; you are establishing the perception that choices create outcomes.

As they grow you can support that notion to develop further. You can ask them "what will that choice create?" and let them discover for themselves, even when neither you nor they know (or believe that you do). And as they get older, and are maybe considering more difficult questions like "Should I go out with this boy?" or debating what subject to study in later education or University, taking the time to sense the wider field of their awareness is a valuable life-skill to develop.

The reality that I operate from is that we are all capable of knowing a great deal more than our cognitive processes will tell us. Many of the greatest businesspeople and investors have an intuitive sense that they use alongside their knowledge. The billionaire George Soros has said openly that his gut-feel is an essential component in his decision-making and I can cite research that backs this up. What might you know that you don't think you know, that if you allowed yourself to know it, would change your life? How might it enhance your child's life to be raised with that perception?

While it is not the subject of this book, this exploration is very much part of my wider writings. My book "The Science of Possibility: Patterns of Connected Consciousness" lays out the science of this new and paradigm-shifting reality. My other offerings that you can discover through the various outlets (Facebook and elsewhere) for "AccesstoPossibility" materials explore the very considerable potential that is available in the "new reality". What becomes possible when you live in the question all of the time? I regard the possibilities as being beyond any limits that we could currently identify. Whether for you or your child, you might wish to explore What else is Possible?

# Biography.  A bit about Jon Freeman

I was a serious child who tried to be an adult too soon.  One parent was a professional musician, the other a teacher and thwarted academic, both careers negatively affected by WW2.

As a teenager I was interested in "how people work", and studied initially Philosophy and Psychology, then Human Sciences, without feeling I got close to satisfactory answers.  After graduating, I became interested in IT, and had a career path from Programmer to Multi-national IT Director to consultant and Programme Manager.  What I enjoyed most was creating and implementing functional applications that helped people do their jobs well and easily.

In the background I began as an emotional incompetent and spent years in self-development of many kinds.  One failed and disastrous marriage (one son, one stepson) and one successful and happy marriage (1 more son) later, I emerged with some grasp of how people function.  But it was a serendipitous encounter with Dr. Don Beck that opened my eyes to the world of Spiral Dynamics, and to how Clare Graves had produced the answers that I would have loved so much to have at university.

The silver lining in that delay was that I didn't become an academic and instead learned about doing real things in the real world.  I am now an organisational development consultant, coach, SDi trainer, writer and communicator producing information like this book, to help expand mind-sets and support others to make their lives better.

My parents were good people who gave me the best of themselves, and sometimes the not-so-great.  No-one had taught them to parent.  I am very grateful for the good parts and have resolved much of the rest.  Through all of my life as described I have been a continual learner and explorer, and this inhabits all that I do.  I have not been a brilliant parent myself; sorry sons.  I believe that learning how to do this job better offers major benefit to the world.  I look forward to sharing that journey.

# Acknowledgements etc.

This book is, as it must be, dedicated to my parents, Dr Jack Massey and Joyce Cordell.

**It does not matter how our parents are. It makes no difference. Life, and all that comes with life, comes to us through them…. There are no more accusations, no blaming. We just take what is given and we turn and let the flow of life pass through us onto the next generation.**

*Bert Hellinger, 2002.*

### *With thanks:-*
To Dr. Clare Graves for the original theory

To Dr. Don E. Beck for the development, the support and the inspiration

To Kelly Isola for opening the opportunity (www.spiralpathways.org)

To Cindy Wigglesworth (www.deepchange.com) for insight and SQ21

To Dr. Veronika Tracy-Smith for expert support and constructive feedback

To Posy Simmonds for the cartoon idea

To Rachel Castagne for sharing the journey in the UK Centre for Human Emergence (www.humanemergence.org.uk)

To the Spiral Dynamics community

To Juliana (www.julianafreeman.co.uk) for sharing the journey of parenthood and my life and to Jack and Yannis for themselves. Also to Glen and Joby for an earlier journey.

**Other resources**

Introductory video produced by the Global Centres for Human Emergence

Spiral Dynamics Intro : https://www.youtube.com/watch?v=JVPIPBRnHnI

Spiral Dynamics Audio box-set by Don Beck (SoundsTrue.com) also available through Audible subscription

You can find information about my certified trainings in Spiral Dynamics on www.spiralfutures.com   These trainings take the basic concepts to full depth, and open up the applications in areas such as Organisational Development, or Leadership and Coaching.

There is a Facebook group Spiral Dynamics Learners through which you can access some free online webinars.

**Other work by Jon Freeman**

Books:-

**"The Science of possibility: Patterns of Connected Consciousness".**

This is a radical new perspective that unifies the scientific and the spiritual views of reality and offers new applications for our ways of being that take us beyond religion and prayer, and into an empowered, intuitive and consciously creative model for human existence.

https://www.amazon.co.uk/Science-Possibility-Jon-Freeman/dp/0956010733

"Reinventing Capitalism, how we broke money and how we fix it, from inside and out"

https://www.amazon.co.uk/Reinventing-Capitalism-broke-Money-inside-x/dp/0956010776

## Adult Personal Development materials:-

This work takes the radical new reality offered by "The Science of Possibility" and unpacks it into a variety of developmental opportunities that open up your choices of how to live. Entry points can be found through the Facebook group AccesstoPossibility or through the website www.accesstopossibility.net

## A variety of articles here:-

https://www.academia.edu/31444905/Whats_the_ANSA_to_VUCA

https://www.academia.edu/34131090/Organisational_Development_Tier_2_Natural_Design_and_Living_Systems_What_does_our_work_call_for

http://www.academia.edu/31444986/The_science_of_homeopathy

http://www.academia.edu/30503553/Out_of_Africa_The_Biological_Ground_of_our_Being

Freeman, J. (2018). A Developmental View of the Personal Psychological Journey. *Journal of Experiential Psychotherapy*, 21 (3), 3-21.

The free-access link to the above article is the following:

https://jep.ro/images/pdf/cuprins_reviste/83_art_1.pdf

Up-to-date information and other articles on www.jonfreeman.co.uk and www.spiralfutures.com

## Autism support

If you are dealing with issues of autism and ADHD, you may find this book offers a supportive perspective that you will not find elsewhere.

"Would You Teach a Fish to Climb a Tree?: A Different Take on Kids with ADD, ADHD, OCD and Autism" by Anne Maxwell (Author), Gary M. Douglas (Author), Dain Heer (Author)

www.ingramcontent.com/pod-product-compliance
Lightning Source LLC
Chambersburg PA
CBHW061703160426
42811CB00090BB/1025